RAVEN REFLECTIONS

A BOOK OF PLACES

J. M. BIRD

Made with ♥ on the Notion Press Platform
www.notionpress.com

To my mother, *Ayesha*.

Contents

Prologue *xi*

1. Anatomy Of Reminiscence – The Places 1
2. Grief Of Remembrance 5
3. Euphoria 7
4. Smile 8
5. Messed Up Thought 9
6. Hate 10
7. Obligation 11
8. Admiration 12
9. Meditation 13
10. Build A Hope 14
11. Worthy Sadness 15
12. Lone Sufferer 16
13. Paradise 17
14. Past I 18
15. Frozen 19
16. Good People 20
17. Ravings I 21
18. Sing 22
19. Us 23
20. Strangers 24
21. Who Might Think About Us? 25
22. A Scene 26
23. A Lament 27

Contents

24. If We Were A Season (title From A Korean Tv Film) 29

25. Fragile 32

26. Sleep 33

27. Flow I 34

28. Stillness 35

29. Adventure 36

30. Hospital Scene 37

31. Past Ii 38

32. Disappeared 39

33. We 40

34. Flow Ii 41

35. Gone 42

36. I 43

37. If Somehow 44

38. Stage 45

39. Absurd 46

40. Let Go 47

41. You 48

42. Be 49

43. Declaration 51

44. Choices 52

45. Character 53

46. Success 54

47. Process 55

Contents

48. People 56

49. Never Settle 57

50. A Wall 58

51. Light 59

52. Longing 60

53. Bad Days 61

54. Three 62

55. Home 63

56. Stereotype 64

57. Ravings Ii 65

58. Sleep 66

59. Despair 67

60. Scene Of A Family 68

61. Family 69

62. A Feeling 70

63. One Morning ... 71

64. Tedium Vitae 72

65. She 73

66. Be Free For A Moment 74

67. Bird 75

68. For A Friend 76

69. Sore Hearts 78

70. Maybe 79

71. You And I 80

Contents

72. Some Days 83

73. Joy 84

74. Questions 85

75. Lonely Lovely ... 86

76. A Moment 87

77. Corruption 88

78. Empty Vase 89

79. Selfless 90

80. Resist 91

81. Opportunity 92

82. Truth 93

83. Child 94

84. I Cannot ... 95

85. Friends 96

86. Them 98

87. Our Spirits 99

88. My Wounds 100

89. Society 101

90. Rejuvenation 102

91. Fears 103

92. Freedom 106

93. Realization 107

94. Growth 108

95. One Thing ... 109

Contents

96. Why? 110

97. Dream 111

98. You Either Care ... 112

99. One Needs God 113

100. Ways 114

101. Rain 115

102. Belief 116

103. Pain 117

104. Women Of House 118

105. Loneliness 119

106. Road 120

107. Lost 122

108. Oblivious 123

109. A Person 124

110. Words 125

111. Love 127

Prologue

Deep into that darkness peering, long I stood there wondering, fearing,
Doubting, dreaming dreams no mortal ever dared to dream before;
But the silence was unbroken, and the stillness gave no token,
And the only word there spoken was the whispered word, "Lenore?"
This I whispered, and an echo murmured back the word, "Lenore!"
Merely this and nothing more.

- The Raven, Edgar Allan Poe

1. Anatomy of Reminiscence – The Places

I visited the family farm and our garden.
One afternoon I felt you around my room,
your long-gone presence - I felt it again.
I walked to the farm: your place
broke a twig from one of many willows there
and sat on the damp ground under a shade.
Sunlight broke the autumn-inflicted foliage,
and the breeze wavered leaves,
sweet warming of my back and heart started.
While I stayed there with nothing to hold on to
I recollected your picture,
took out my cell phone, and peeked at its wallpaper.
Your lips carried a fond smile.
I recollected your walk in the thicket,
amidst the trees, so proud and lively standing their ground.
The twig I broke became my *miswak*.
I listened to the wind going around me,
felt the rustle of the leaves,
and watched them fall.
I heard some children jest in the distance.

I took in the chorus that defines the autumn in Kashmir-
the cicadas- their continuous shrill, resonating all the visible landscape.
One landed on a tree next to me,
but did not make any noise,
just lingered there for a moment and took off silently.
Then the old blue-whistling-thrush,
ever-alone thrush of the past.
It lurked there on the pole for a minute: sulking,
noticing the changing color of leaves, the yellow rising deeply.
It too took off with a gentle flap: like a tired heartbeat. No songs.
I loitered a few more minutes there on the damp ground,
thinking about the past,
listening to our togetherness lingering there.
"But you ain't no more here to see all this",
no matter how much time the world goes on,
you will never come back: "here to this place".
I know that and the place knows that,
and the universe knows that.
Maybe this is what we are meant to do,
roam the places, make them ours,
then disappear, vanish from the stage,
leave the places to others,
let them cater to memories and stays of new faces,
let new souls replace the old ones.
An everlasting process, ever continuous,

repeating itself with us, through us,
like a river entering the same ocean again and again.
And this is how we return to the places; through the same places,
as you return to me every day,
as you returned to me that afternoon in the garden.
I stood a few more moments,
and tried to picture you here and there-
standing under the shade,
watering the collard,
nibbling an apple on the grass,
collecting dandelion.
I tried all other memories, bad or good:
the late sunsets,
the bird-watching,
discussions on their migration,
mowing of grass,
tomatoes to slake the thirst in mid-summer-afternoon,
our arguments on the viability of pesticides,
their toxicity imbibed in every natural element,
and other moments that were immaterial to me then,
and that is everything to me now.
Maybe this is how you are living now,
in the fields and moors that surround me,
the old mountains you trekked to get firewood,
the streets you walked your whole life,
the same cold breeze I feel now,

the quiet places you loved to sojourn,
the chirp of birds-
all this might be you touching my inscape,
leaking feelings,
loving me.
all is maybe you. even I. I am you.

2. Grief of Remembrance

I remember
the mornings you would make breakfast and pack our lunch, wave goodbye, and bless us;
the longing to be by our side anytime we would leave to spend the day;
your face in that perfect moment waiting for us at the door;
the look, the fidgets that would take over your calm whenever we would be late;
the laughs we shared, the deep conversations we inspired.
I remember:
how you would hold us with love, stroke some long hair, or caress a face, and the relief that would spread through;
the days you nourished us back to joy; sheltered the ailing spirits with your umbrella of love.
I remember
your love for life, for the blue sky of spring, the East wind of morning; your affection for the countryside, or a child;
the late evenings we would marvel at the sky, the stars and their constellations, the shooting meteors, and how I would explain to you their science, quell your curiosity, and how we both would laugh at the complexity of it.
You were the sky of a late evening, with a lone star, twinkling, warning against the dark of night, guiding a lost one home;

you were the midnight sky full of stars that would fill a soul with wonders, dreams, and hope- that even the darkest times harbor scintillations of light.
You were the sky of the full moon, soft beams of which would shine upon a darkening room;
you were the sky of the sun, keeping life joyous.
Now it is dark, heavens shut us out, you are gone, we feel homeless.

3. Euphoria

(a song by BTS)

the euphoria of the past slowly burns into the dysphoria, of the present…
the song is on a loop and you feel something beating for nothing…
nothing you see around no laughter or a touch…
you fall out of a cradle,
a cradle of false joy reaching out to you from the past…
you cry cause memories come hard on you, dysphoria …
"shouldn't the world end?"
you end up in the euphoria of being with memory again;
in nothingness maybe…
the joy of desire to lie together in a place you call heaven…
you seek togetherness in one room of the home where life passes quickly…
you keep the song on loop walking deep into a sad wasteland.

4. Smile

you need to look at yourself –
in the mirror, I mean – and smile back.
practice making it a part of your lips as long as you have a life to live.
it could lead you to another smiling soul,
you know – a smile keeps another smile.

5. Messed up thought

all the messed-up heads know –
there ain't nothing that could love them back
the way a moment of not giving a F does.
the word ain't anything but an idea…

6. Hate

chew your tongue
and give it an injury
for all the words that ruined a moment.
let it be a reminder – if it suffices.
to hate is a try at something that earns nothing.
but sometimes a crack in the wall gives the light a chance to get rid of the dark.
sometimes hate becomes the answer –
things falling apart, then coming together with new life and force... but unlike love, hate has no eternity – it cannot sustain, a thing with no eternity suffices nothing.

7. Obligation

An obligation to pretend - a smile on the face,
an okay attitude,
a fake facade, just because you think "people need your smile"
-
but they need truth, bad truth.
death ain't any bad truth,
you could die right now.
you need to be conscious about it as much as you are about life.
an obligation to have death in mind - could have an impact
...

8. Admiration

I believe,
we all admire -
a self, an image, an idea -
there ain't a moment without grace,
when a face, a person you imagine, and admire.

9. Meditation

There is something about life that makes it complicated,
something undesirable to live.
you meditate on a dream or a desire of which you become a liver.
it keeps you awake and consumes your will, yet you ain't ready to cave in.
"maybe being in the shoes of ignorance was better,
walk streets like a dolt, laughing or crying for nothing – act stupid,
let pleasure conquer senses"
but the pain never lets it happen.
comes back - the sleep of pain brings comfort.
comfort is a lie - reality is a nightmare, it is a list of your fears.

10. Build a Hope

love without limits.
keep loved ones close to heart,
to stay human
to not be an outsider
to not let adversity get you
to channel emotions
to build a hope -
in a beloved.

11. Worthy Sadness

not pleasure
but a worthy sadness makes life sweet –
after that – “sad people always find a way to stay sad.”

12. Lone Sufferer

you be part of my joy
I'm a lone warrior
and deserve suffering for my choices.
you be part of my smile, I'm a lone sufferer.

13. Paradise

ain't any dreamland,
or a place beyond the skies
or an unfathomable landscape –
it is a Smiling Face spreading Hope,
that is a paradise.

14. Past I

No.

Peace ain't nowhere in today or tomorrow.

It resides in certain pasts.

In memories.

Reminiscing is a blissful state.

Today or tomorrow – a mere formality.

15. Frozen

to write,
about everything that makes life.
to write – what do you feel?
what do you see? how?
figure out.
right now – you are frozen,
a beach without sunset,
an ocean without life, a shore without waves.

16. Good People

good people – deserve a good life – crap
– deserve good suffering – unwise
– deserve love – lie
– deserve a chance to do bad with no repercussions – worth a struggle.

17. Ravings I

we walk a path to talk.
we pray for a friend to listen to,
to say things to.
we let a feeling create a void inside,
dream of evading moments,
wounds of words –
take out all,
talk guilt, waste, anguish, defeat –
talk everything – it is okay.
talk about what is in-between mind and heart –
things we don't think about, or desire,
dead dreams we obsess over.
oh! a dream – to join you – wherever you are.
life gets you – you want to quit – dream to be you.
lone lights of nights of eternal autumn pushing spring far.
people of tomorrow – a conscious machine.
have an emptiness to vent.
have dry sand to spread.
a tree in autumn.
no spring in sight – the great fall.

18. Sing

know and sing about –
the truth we hide from –
complexity devouring us,
modernity misunderstood,
mad vices glamorized.
know and sing about –
false gods and ideas,
political hypocrisy,
manipulators of society,
captors of happiness,
oppressors of oppressed,
dividers of faith,
killers of a land.
know and sing about you,
protest imperial delusions.
resist, and sing about resistance.

19. Us

what separates us?
I feel us only when I feel death.
on the other side of life, is it your calling?
is life an obstruction to the union?
or all this is a delusion?
no you or I. only us.

20. Strangers

away from home,
I walk strange streets,
I observe strange strangers,
the unrequited love in their eyes,
sold to wants and greed.

21. Who might think about us?

who might think about us?
in the cold rain of September, think about our whereabouts.
as they pass by our graveyard.
will they think about how we ended up there?
will they know of despair?
that came from an unfulfilled desire to tame happiness in her youth.
will they know about our cracked tongues shunning truth?
will they judge us for our falsehood?
I wonder.

22. A scene

out in the fields of mustard,
into the thin spring air,
I spoke words
of love, of freedom, of solitude,
and about a lone bird striving against a high breeze in that still sky,
flying on and on,
leaving beneath the earth of humans.
I felt the soft soaring wind wavering mustard bloom,
I felt the joy of it for lovers of nature, solitude, pain,
passing hours in serene land,
longing for some unknown sail across the still river of life
to some paradise
like a stray child reaching an embrace of Mother.

23. A lament

Once in autumn I wandered around in lonesome air and sat heedlessly in a graveyard under a chinar that struck me with its autumnal attire.

It sang to me the autumnal melancholy, so, I reclined pensively under it my beaten self to wait for Thee.

Reposed against its bark, I gave myself to dreams, to fancy my dark heart illuminated by Godly Gleams.

Ah! How to dream not of you and I evening walking our childhood pasture, holding our hands in love, rejoicing our leisure.

I sat there relaxed with harbored ease and longed for us to freeze somewhere up on our childhood lands of peace where the sight of azure would release us from these sorrows and sufferings, these materialistic cages, emancipate us from holding corrupt rules of corrupt sages.

Sweet me! Thousand moments and more passed under the Chinar tree, and I felt my bruised heart craving for Thee.

My eyes were glued to our often-walked path but you my beloved appeared not.

I walked a few yards in silence to touch the mossy turf of the nearby grave and shuddered beneath the yellow soar shelter that Chinar to dead gave.

Time knew no passing, no length, and I had nothing but to wait for Thee, Thine Soul I prayed to be.
Pangs of pain took my fibers of heart when all of sudden my coward boy of your death thought.
Just the dreadful thought of you my life dying, I broke there and still lamenting the thought I am all my soul crying.
I sighed and prayed for your arrival like the rain of mid-June, to drench me in love and nourish my ruin.
Good came when I lost self to the graveyard silence, gave up my heart to it, to lull its violence. It took from dead their unshed tears and nothing but yearned for you to end its day nightmares.
As a weak, wimpish, withering child parted from Mother, I cried till I was empty, till eyes dried to cruelty, till I found me loathe, you for abandoning me as such.
And such I reveled in the quiet our memories of past and faltered more to shed the unshed, and laid miserably myself on the mossy turf of nearby grave to feel forlorn heart dead.

24. If we were a season (title from a Korean TV film)

1.
If we were a season – you and I
we could pass with no regrets maybc,
we could just slightly be in touch for a while
and leave with memories and goodbyes
never afraid of some emotion jamming our hearts.
2.
If we were seasons – I spring and you autumn
I- winter and you- summer
we could bring so many colors
so many birds along
a new breeze harboring new life
love that we could share will have the imminence of change with it
not slave to the idea of a single feeling.
3.
If we were seasons – we shall never long for togetherness
or hope for the world to keep us happy
or miss each other for too much time
we shall live in uncertainty.

4.

If we were a season –
white in winter, yellow in fall,
green in spring, and warm in summer,
love for us could bless all
if we were a season or seasons.

5.

If we were a season or seasons – you and I,
changing and chasing new colors around the year
sometimes catching up but just a caress,
breathing no animosity for abandoning each other,
if we were in different seasons chasing each other.

6.

If we were a season – temporary but repeating
the joy we pray to have for eternity might just have been a moment or a phase
of a defining momentary union.

7.

If we were a season – the hot salty tears burning us to ashes
could become a summer rain,
the goodbyes could just be a talk to see each other again.

8.

If we were a season – returning, again and again,
to find ourselves with new lives.

9.

what if we were just a day in a season?
the day is too long – say a moment,

a moment of evening chill in winter
bringing lovers together under a hung evening moon.
or a spring morning minute,
waking people to a green hope.
or a summer afternoon when friends collide with bottles of water.
or a minute of an autumnal evening when walkers see the sun going down and feel the time passing them.

10.

If we were a season – pass with no guilt and regret
whether it is order or chaos we bring together,
no good or bad memory – just memory,
impressing some sensitive souls.
no goodbyes,
no fears of some mechanized emotion jamming us,
if we were a season or seasons chasing each other.

25. Fragile

hold me!
I'm fragile
like a hung leaf of a tree in the autumn
vulnerable to a gentle breeze left for the winter.

26. Sleep

who could understand that
sleep doesn't always mean peace?
it could relate to an unbearable tiresome escape
from life pouring in its weary traditions.
Life must be different from death
but could you relate to an idea that
maybe the whole life is actually death in process –
it ain't an abrupt cessation of breathing
but something that takes place over years as you age
maybe life is dying –
I guess there is no life – no living force
but dying force – one that keeps us here.
to die after decades or some minutes
that is why we are here.

27. Flow I

I need to be anything that flows like water.
You know, not anything viscous like humans.

28. Stillness

I still live the same way as a child
except now I dream less and act more.
And I made a deal with time to love and live till the day there is nothing to love and live.

29. Adventure

happiness, whenever felt, leaves us an afterword of a sad story. whether we are living or dying, our search for something higher than simple existence keeps us grounded to the ground.
what is life but a multitude of thoughts put into action?
what are we but different reflections in the same mirror?
when you sleep, intend to dream about flights to the horizon, of every other lively adventure and one day live every one of them with no regret.

30. Hospital scene

As I lay on a waiting bench with a tired heart, desperate spirits, thirsty throat, dead mind, and grieving eyes – a girl child laughed a beautiful laugh when her father played with her messy hair. The air around her rejoiced. Hope in a place that reeked of hopeless medicine and half-dead people. God existed in her at the moment.

31. Past II

Some bad shit about the past keeps you awake at night, right? I need you to keep it in your heart and remind yourself of the bad you are capable of doing, but I also need you to let go of it when the morning comes. A new day means new possibilities. Hang on to that destructive idea of hope. There is no other way.

32. Disappeared

When you left, I stopped desiring to be at the top of the ladder.
When you left, hierarchy disappeared, competition sucked, and I started navigating life for the sake of living.

33. We

Only when there is no You and I
when what separates Us becomes our reason for union, you can feel satisfaction peeping in.
It is with We and Us, we can know life and feel it.

34. Flow II

Flow regardless of the obstructions.

Believe in your transcendence and search for something beyond what you are feeling about this wrecked ship world.

35. Gone

I am long gone from your life.
I was your sad face and you are somewhere safe and happy now. I know.
I was your hopeless thought that kept you sleepless and now you are somewhere free and thoughtless. You are out there not to survive but to thrive with joy, with bliss.
I was winter morning rain you hated, now I am gone from your winters and you are somewhere seasonless.
You are heart within me, thriving and alive, and I know you are somewhere beyond this mundanity. I need to reach you, need you to stop beating inside me and let me end. I know, at the end of this road you are with open arms and smiling face, waiting.

36. I

You will not find me ambitious.

You will find me passionate about life.

About small things.

Like smiling at strangers in street, and playing with kids.

You will find me longing for morning walks, sunsets, some drinks, and dinners with family.

You will find my heart full of now, empty of caring about tomorrow and matured constantly by revisiting yesterday rights and wrongs.

And I have a habit of killing my mood repeatedly for people I love. I have made loving people my priority.

37. If somehow

If we could somehow reunite and get our time back, I would hold you close, and never let you slip away.
I would bind my soul to you with love.
So that separation won't be a choice.

38. Stage

At a certain stage in life, you leave bothering about things – you realize submission doesn't mean giving up to the will of people and letting them control you – submission means to find God – the One who knows where submission will take you.

You realize that whatever happens, happens – good is in accepting the evil and striving against it – evil is not absolute like good. At a certain stage in life, you start examining things from God's perspective – you start harmonizing the animal in you with something good – you give up worrying about expectations, love, hate, jealousy, pride, arrogance, wealth, health – you start actualizing 'nothingness' – a stage where everything comes out of nothing and returns to nothing – because everything is just an utterance of God.

At this point, you worry about blind beliefs manifested by yearning to be superior in the world. you realize every sin takes you to the doors of Allah. suffering is better than ease that paves the way to the slumps of self-adornment. you start to despise the weak will of a human – vacillation between carnal desires and spiritual needs. you start examining your deeds – your SELF.

39. Absurd

It takes all life out of me – when the stupidity of existence hits me. We have to fade out eventually from each other's memories we may never see the same view again yet we hope to have all the absurd.

40. Let go

Let go of whatever is holding you back – embrace whatever keeps you driven. hatever keeps you awake at night.

41. You

You are not a sponge.

You cannot let their negative energy dampen you.

You need to be above all the little nuisances of the day.

So much of life is already wasted on trivial stuff like what happens tomorrow.

Tomorrow is a prison – now is your key.

You be either prisoner of tomorrow or king of the present.

42. Be

Be worthy of whatever you are going through.
Be eternal.
Be ephemeral.
Never die.
Never live.
Be everything.
Be nothing.
Be a paradox.
Be an ambiguity that way they can't get you.
So, don't let them get you.
Laugh like you have never cried.
Live like the meaninglessness of life is the meaning.
be limitless in everything:
good – bad.
life – death.
love – hate.
See where it takes you.
don't try to be happy.
Just be happy.
Happiness is an attitude.
It shouldn't always come from the surroundings.
But it should always come from within you.

So, be who you are and see who stays.
You be brave.
So much that life cowers before you.
You be on the watch.
You live your every day thinking this is the opportunity Allah has given you and you can be anything.
Because as always - you are unique,
you are beautiful.
No matter what the world says - you be unique,
You be beautiful.

43. Declaration

My discomfort – I never got a fair opportunity to do what I do best. Now I shall give my life to be what I need to be. now I need no support. now I know the ropes and how to pull them.

44. Choices

Sometimes in life, we make choices out of compulsion. We do not feel compassionate or loving about ourselves for what we do. We just try to do it for the sake of escape. This is when we are vulnerable to failure. What you do should come from within – like an aquifer – it should come out like a light from the sun. Only then there is a chance of a majestic rise after a steep fall.

45. Character

develop a character where it won't be a matter of concern to you whether people add to your happiness or not. you should be your happiness. you should be your peace.

46. Success

We could do better. Live better. Shun the greed for comfort. Instead, accept the situations and grow. Life never treats cowards with respect. It throws them to chaos. Whether you achieve what you need from life or not – does not matter as much as your will to fight, your resolve to make it a purpose. keep running after it until you become success – until your definition of success comes into existence

47. Process

Don't know how to make others understand but I feel a new thought process taking shape in me lately. A state of mind where winning, losing, success or failure – this dichotomy loses meaning. I feel the meaninglessness of all these aspects or call standards of life - somehow, I try to understand "the meaning of meaninglessness". One thing matters – the process. What brings all the grinding out of you?

Life cannot be rigid. It always gives new perspectives and meanings. It gives joy as well as sorrow. And the meaning resides in living the sorrow, the melancholy – of living on even if you don't want to. But you realize you need to. It is more about breathing in the stench of a decomposing carcass without disgust.

48. People

Your decisions are going to affect people around you. And they are surely going to talk about you. But whatever it is they say, let it go. Don't overdo it. Don't overthink or over-feel it. Be numb. Act stupid. If that is what it takes to escape the pain that their words cause. Harness every bad word and ponder over it to up the ante against whatever it is you are doing and climb your mountain. Trust the process and don't care what they are going to say about your decisions.

49. Never settle

It is okay to lose a day if it pushes you to win a month. Never settle for a 'give up' attitude.

Not the world, it is yourself you need to conquer. Everything will follow – even the peace you seek.

Every fall is part of a divine plan to make your rise elegant and memorable.

Losing hope or giving up is cowardice.

The only braveness I know is to smile – no matter what befalls you.

The problem stops being a problem when you learn to take it as an opportunity to grow.

"Focus. Fear. Fly" always come back – restart every day with newness.

50. A wall

Should I be telling you about a wall I seem to be climbing but never making it to the top ever since the day I was born?
It is like a sea stonewalling a river if it demands separate existence. There are no ways to walk out when things are done out of necessity. There ain't any good answers to why things are the way they are. We have limited experience with things we think we master. There ain't nothing like mastery. We all are children playing around.

51. Light

You float like plastic in the sea to nowhere from somewhere.

That is how you feel life is going …

But you are different actually…

You are a fish chasing light.

You need to know that above-ocean fish cannot survive.

Choose your light wisely.

Sometimes it is good to be in darkness.

Just to survive an hour or more.

Light will reach you someday.

52. Longing

I have a longing heart.
One that never grieves or rejoices.
A longing only – to break – and become new.
Shed what I have been engineered to think.
Longs for love – from the Source of Love.
I have a longing heart.
One that knows no sorrow or joy.
Longs for a dream – to be free of all attachments, and indifferent to all sufferings.
Have God as my purpose.
Nothing else is a concern but this longing.

53. Bad days

Some mornings – life will kill you.

Actually, kill your spirits.

You wake up with tired feelings and vanquished spirits.

And you pray for a long sleep.

Such days are difficult to start with a smile or hope of a new start.

On such mornings – revel in the hopelessness of the moment.

Don't hesitate to feel the pain.

Live for the sake of mundane existence – just exist. Exist and know that the next day will be better.

54. Three

1.

Life fades.

As time goes by and you count the years.

You feel yourself fading away, hiding in a box far from your reach.

As you plan you feel life fading; you feel vibes of approaching death; things you never cared about suddenly start becoming meaningful.

2.

The thing about being unapologetically unhappy is that people don't expect you to make them happy. People who are ready to take you to a stage where you can enjoy doing what you love to do – keep those people close. They matter lifetime.

3.

The problem is not suffering. The problem is our refusal to suffer. We refuse to suffer – that is where the whole problem of life not being fair starts.

55. Home

1.

They say home is a feeling.

And I need to build myself a home.

Can we build a feeling? Is it possible?

2.

I feel alive when I imagine you writing to me or saying my name like you belong to some home I have built in my dreams.

This mad awareness returns.

56. Stereotype

I think it breaks like a vase holding flowers,
spill all decorations, and is full of mess and longing. Longing
to be whole again and to have a self-made decorum.
For to unmake the made is the dream I dream,
the journey I need to take the living I call living:
I cannot live the stereotype.

57. Ravings II

I feel tears sting, a necessity to cry,
longing to be held by you.
I feel heartache, pain wringing out bliss.
I feel the urge to truckle,
never raise my voice or write a word,
be numb to the outside world,
take refuge in the quietude of early morning or late night,
tranquil my agitations.
Living is an abnormality that keeps me from being with you for an eternity.
I feel something deep stirring inside me,
feeding me with indifference to everything out there. I feel for the boy who died of a bullet alone on the streets with no warmth but cold death.

58. Sleep

I need sleep to dream,
defy gravity,
and have my tears wrung out by the blue sky of dreams.
I need life to know dying before death,
to know the secrets of pain,
to know sad spirits go through me again and again.

59. Despair

we carry despair to anger to hate,
we build walls of war,
we are groups destined to ruin,
we are foam falling apart,
we are cold hearts with warm parts,
pouring acid rain,
we are fine scavengers like we are.

60. Scene of a family

dandelion-strewen high grass we danced over
a game of badminton we talked over
a mother of a family laughed over the insanities and vanities of youth.
a mother of a family watched over her children one last time
laughed for them one last time
loved them one last time
and then died for them one last time.

61. Family

1.

beautiful sun,
never ache in June,
never let the breeze go,
never abandon us to a night,
ever leave us to wolves of winter.
beautiful sun,
stay over us evermore.

2.

all tears in the world are shed for a broken home.
all tears in worlds come for a yearn to be inside a familial perfection to be loved for good.

62. A feeling

I feel you as scald feels run of cold water.
I live you as a mother lives her child. be to me what fragrance is to a flower.

63. One morning ...

One April morning, I took a chair in the yard. Ruminated over some symbols and images for a poem I needed to write.

A bee buzzed beneath the chair.

Pollen forager of some hive.

I felt instant inspiration.

An emotion was lit inside me.

The incredible pace of the bee.

How it took each flower perfectly.

It cut me deep; the intense joy of work the bee must be experiencing.

How atrophic we have grown with our desire to sit still in comfort.

To kill days on the work we hate to do.

So that we could have stashes of currency.

I pitied myself.

64. Tedium vitae

what is worth an education that doesn't give you choice;
the choice to choose between head and heart.
but maybe all we are here for is to break our hearts on repeat,
make heartbreaking choices and come to terms with *tedium vitae* - a disinterested but calm life.
this is how a tasteless savor the taste of life,
by living off the pleasure of sensations until the senses forsake and educate him about impermanence.
that is how we realize why breaking ourselves is necessary.
why it matters for us to grow beyond animals?
such awareness matters -
as a thrush matters to a composed morning
a companion matters in a desert
the moon matters to the night
the green matters to the spring
God matters to a believer
life matters to death
suffering matters to a calm heart.

65. She

1.

some people are born with divine boats.
they keep them from sinking into the waters of the worldly gloom.
she was one of them.
sorrow was always too shallow to drown a creation like her.
she would always smile and walk on.

2.

there was so much certainty and faith in her prayer. it could have made dead rise from their graves had she prayed for it.

3.

she goes out that door - she goes on,
walking towards a place she had made for herself,
she had let me go.

4.

she stood there alone in the moment and I glowed over her, taking-in her grace.
she was beautiful in the moment and I was happy to have her in the moment – just for me.

66. Be free for a moment

I sense the lonely nights and days spent figuring out ways "in pursuit of happiness".
look around and step out of your caged heart,
shed the burden of expectations for a moment,
be free,
immerse into your sea,
let waves toss and rush your shore,
and feel your life kissing your gentle core.
keep your heart calm,
and let go of the bitter past.
lose yourself to the vastness of life.
you won't stay here forever,
your trail is memories you leave,
put your faith in God - let Him take care of things you left uncared.

67. Bird

I wish to breathe out this Bird in me,
and watch my beloved cage fall,
to the silence of the earthy dark.
how come dead brave,
the despair of dark,
of lonely cold nights,
of mocking crawl of worms,
no sun, no moon, no stars,
just a dark strange Void,
looming.
what am I?
A human confused - bleeding torment,
a beating heart,
a naught in space,
or them!
I'm them! I'm the Law!
corrupted!
I try to live my bird,
my dove,
but they cut my wings!
but I will crawl-fly. Yes.

68. For a friend

Come along as you are now.
Be forever like this.
Let me not break.
Hold me with your words, your laughter.
With your smile, your talk.
We lose time.
Be my hope.
Keep me close to your world.
Shall I write what I love in you?
How do I miss our time?
I will burn nights with no other thing but ink and paper.
Give me momentary bliss.
Hold me now and then till time keeps us entangled.
In this sweet entanglement of the worldly maze -cruel forgetfulness! how friendships fade!
I remember every moment.
All I do sometimes is meditate over you.
I remind me of your generosity.
Till there is a world and in it there is you and there is me, love shall never die.
God knows what tomorrow will bring!
A grave or a long road to some stale boring life.
So, I pray for your company - to be on some endless journey

with you.
I will write more about us about days of togetherness.

69. Sore hearts

should sore hearts rejoice in the coming prized autumn?
or be loyal to leaving summer that could be dying eternal?
thus, goes life we so dearly and desperately hold on to,
while minds keep us mundane, hearts strive to be divine,
while we keep desiring inhibition of the autumn and eternity of the spring,
God leads us to a destination – a world with no season – an eternal upbringing.

70. Maybe

1.

maybe all the things I did in life nullify all the other things I didn't even try.
or maybe it is otherwise.
thoughts are always in crisis.

2.

maybe sadness nowadays is too deep for us and there is no other way but to pretend - pretend that you are happy, I am happy and the world is happy.
maybe we shouldn't mope around like kids anymore and suck up things - no matter what.

71. You and I

1.

you rose over me like the moon,
now nights are soft and smooth.
I feel blunt and numb like dead,
then you come up in me and everything turns into life again.

2.

out of all walks, I miss the ones I took with you
when the space between us was filled with smiles and dreams of togetherness
when life was with us.

3.

no matter where the world stands I always stand with you.

4.

you are a breathing hope that there is still something in the world to look at with a smile on my face.

5.

the beautiful thing about you is your ability to prefer- love over hate, hope over fear, and life over death.

6.

a part of yours clung to mine,
something deep from your soul went deep into mine and I felt it and absorbed it
like a sponge.

I feel damp now.
a damp figure holding onto some eternal words of hope.
but in actuality, there ain't anything to hold on to except the memory of your touch.

7.

I can disappear and you won't ever hear from me if that is what you need, not want.

8.

you know what – I think you will live.
you will live to witness something beautiful and lovcly.
you just need to hold on to your lovely self.
hold on to whatever you find hopeful.

9.

there was so much to say and so little time
that silence felt like the answer to every question and question to every answer.

10.

I hold a person in my heart, and I live repeatedly a life in lone memory.

11.

you stood there on the bank watching me rowing
I prayed to have you by my side -
to have your hands in mine to wade through troubled waters
and you stood there like a fading star.
I went on rowing against the viscous sea,
it all ended in fatigue spirits and I stopped cutting water and stood stuck there in the middle of the sea. we made two stones

of us watching each other- and the world moved on while we stood glued to something that was never ours.

72. Some days

some days you are tired,
your soul is so vanquished that you pray for the night to never end,
the morning to never break-
you pray for endless sleep.

73. Joy

There is joy in doing something that hits you in the guts and gives you a feeling that you are alive even if that something is nothing to the world.

74. Questions

1.

have you ever felt an emotion a human touch could light in you?
not a physical touch but something abstract like a blank stare.

2.

how much do we waste ourselves?
nothing compared to the false life we live with a demoralized purpose.

75. Lonely lovely ...

it is late evening.
it is drizzling.
and I am on the roads.
alone.
taking in the darkest night that is dawning.
cell phone repeatedly plays a death song and I am swaying to it.
there ain't any soul out here.
just some flickering street lights.
I am a lonely soul swaying to a death song.
and I am a lonely lovely soul on lovely earth.

76. a moment

first breathe it in then live a moment.
we never live.
we always die.
but anyways live, no matter how.

77. Corruption

I need to bloody bleed this corruption in me.
This lazing around with life.
This parasitic desire for comfort.
I need to bleed this greed.

78. Empty vase

I am a vase.
An empty vase.
No flowers.
I receive water from the tap.
We make a lot of noise together.
Water filling is unbearable.
It is impossible to not grunt or wince.
I feel like it might wear me out.
But I hold on.
And wait.
Something happens when water overflows and touches the tap.
Silence happens.
It takes over the bloody noise I had to bear.
That's how we grow silent.
Together.
"Time's constant drip wears a human out.
He/she feels filled.
Filled with liquids of passion that the world serves cold.
Tap is world – man an empty vase."

79. Selfless

Sometimes act so much selfless that your Self craves you.
"Cause happiness".
Be "felicific".

80. Resist

Because there is a thing called resistance.

I resist therefore I exist.

Resist every shifty character life puts you with.

81. Opportunity

We have an opportunity here to shun life and embrace death, to let go of the fear and live the way death wants us to.

82. Truth

1.

It hurts when you see things in the light of truth.

But it sets you on the right course.

It breaks you and broken is better than false bliss.

2.

When we fail to create anything as impactful as life.

We create ways to kill it.

We give them names like school, job, sleep, marriage, and so on.

3.

Give them truth and they will defend it with justified lies. then they ignore you.

83. Child

So, a child is born.
Lovely to hold.
Cute and soft. I look at it and I feel like a hapless creature.
Like I'm born again.
It occurs to me how its life is going to be a shade of others already swarming the place.
How its life is going to be shaped by society.
How schools will condition its life.
So much that everything normal will become abnormal.
Then dictation of right and wrong.
Make it look black and white.
Make out of it someone who worships society.
"There is no god but society and money is its messenger."
Nobody will define the strength of character to the child.
If it turns out to be someone sensitive - a person who observes and thinks, it shall remake itself.
Or it might just be another addition to their collective unconsciousness.
Or it may turn into another hopeless wanderer?

84. I cannot ...

1.

I cannot belong here.

Even if I compromise with their idea of life, I would be a dead soul dragging itself to the door of death.

2.

There are moments when everything becomes blurred.

You see yourself like a white dot on a black slate as if only you exist.

That is when I pray to lose myself.

3.

There is nothing good to hold on to in me.

I always see it in others and cling to it.

85. Friends

They are not friends if they get tired of your craziness.
If they become selective about your behavior when it comes to spending time with you.
If they start taking you as a failure and gone case.
If they don't get along with your madness.
They are not friends if they replace you when they find blues with you.
If they find you tired of the hackneyed life you lead with them and instead of trying to have a life back into your friendship, they abandon you.
They are not friends if they make you feel that you don't belong with them.
They are only friends if they let you be the same self they found you at the start.
If they let you grow the way you need to grow.
If they correct you for your sake.
If they hold on to the smiles you shared and tears you wiped together.
They are friends if they see you in themselves.
They are friends if together you feel spiritual.
If together a plaintive nod breaks them into laughter. Friendship means having something to do together and being each other's home when the world fits no longer as home.

A good friendship has creative and productive ways of escapism.
It means to have friends with whom life itself is a means of escape from a bad going.
It means to stay sad together and make out of togetherness a memorable moment.
It means an order to your chaos.

86. Them

1.

Sometimes it is better to give them what they never expect.
Most of the time it is better to just ignore them.
Often it is good to let them think they are in control.
And then take them to a point where they are ready to accept you for who you are.

2.

If you want people to stay out of your life matters, let them underestimate you. The few that deserve to be in your life would never let you feel underestimated and you will know the difference between people in the first line and the few in the third line.

3.

You are left with three choices:
be vulnerable, observe how people treat you, and act accordingly;
pretend to be strong and callous and build a shell around you;
be both and take the middle path and be with few people who know both sides.

87. Our spirits

What keeps us grounded in life?
What keeps us hooked to the melancholy of life?
What makes us do anything to keep going in this world of absurdities?
Maybe love: of life, of self, of family, of being the best version.
Love of money, fame, and passionate partner.
We are drunk on the idea that we deserve love.
But maybe humans are enough into the mud of shame that they don't deserve love anymore.
We failed God.
But there could be a resurrection.
We could look for it in love again.
In places where life breathes redemption.
We are loners in the world and we are our own company.
We may not find what we need but we cannot give up searching.
Searching is surge our spirits need.

88. My wounds

I stood beneath the gloom of the grey sky and asked myself "what brought you the wounds you have now?" "You want to be loved, listened and admired."

89. Society

The thought of living a societal-appreciated "normal" was a disease society admired.

It gave them the momentary security and peace that comes with lies.

90. Rejuvenation

Nothing in this world could stop you from doing what you are meant to do.

You cannot let the world's rub reduce you to a sack. You need rejuvenation.

You need to take a new path.

You need a new birth.

You need a new spirit.

You need YOU.

91. Fears

1.

You obviously fear reputation.
We all do.
Always take steps with plans.
Always try to control life as if we can.
We don't think about how unpredictable life is.
How one could wake up alive and die the minute s/he opens his eyes?
We never want to see our plans falling apart.
Maybe we don't consider our insignificance in a vast universe.
Every risk counts. Every failure counts.
People laugh-
well, know that there is always someone who talks and laughs when you take a different path.
What matters is how ready you are to take everything on your knees.
Never let their opinion disturb your peace.
You keep going like the sun.
No matter what happens you shall always rise with a smile and set with majesty.

2.

World out there has somewhere in its center made it a goal to discommode individuals who think differently and try to do

things in a different way.
So, don't let it disturb your waters.
Be calm. Be a stone to your own waters and create your own ripples. Don't give people enough power to disturb your calm sea.

3.

At some point in life, you may notice a few close ones replacing you.
Replacing you because you stood up for yourself.
You finally started listening to yourself and stopped pleasing them. You finally learned to say no and it didn't go well with them.
They can't see you living for yourself.
Perhaps they loved to see you looking for happiness in them.
Perhaps it made them feel special.
But you need to feel special too.
So, be yourself and be better without them.

4.

Sometimes bad things happen for something good. Look out for each bad incident in life no matter how small it may be.
Every time you suffer, there is a chance to start life anew.
Desire, and dish out to yourself the newness you wish to see every time you suffer.

5.

Do not ever fear adversity of standing up for yourself. It won't kill you unless you let it. What could possibly happen if you go against the demands of society? You run the risk of being in psychic agony if you give up on yourself. Don't let fear of life or death make you miserable.

92. Freedom

When you realize that nothing matters because everything matters,
you reach a new level of freedom with new certainty.

93. Realization

We realize this shit very late in our lives that in places like Kashmir, everything gets old with time.

Love, hate, life, death … everything grows old.

Nothing moves you the way it moves you the first time. Every damn thing stales.

Failure, success, suffering, or happiness – all lose meaning. You turn into a personified acceptance – ready for every facet of life.

Everything becomes nothing and after some more time - nothing becomes everything.

94. Growth

Glad tidings self - now you are more tamed and less wild, less dreamy and more real, less happy and sadder less new and more old.

Now you are more efficacious and less alive.

95. One thing ...

There are times when people say stuff to you – make you feel useless and shit.
But remember one thing: "I would rather sit back in a room and die of starvation than go out there just to eat and reproduce like a rabbit."

96. Why?

What went wrong that we are so far from us?
What killed life between us?
What brought separation to us?
Lost now.
What happened to a sad home together?
What happened to embracing dark side?
What happened to loving selflessly?
Why so much pain inside?
Why not let things go?
Why be this much considerate about something that is not even ours?
Why not be yourself again?
Why care about things so much?
Why give life a direction when it is better directionless?
Why keep looking for a lost treasure?
Why not just exist and move on?
Why not fade out like morning star?
Fade out repeatedly every morning.

97. Dream

I have a dream to have no dream at all, to wade through nothingness and reach some placelessness.

98. You either care ...

You either care too much or you don't care at all. There is no middle path.

99. One needs God

Some bad years of life are enough to give you this realization that to have contentment, one needs God - one has to move to a stage where s/he knows deep in her/his guts that God is always there.

And no damn thing will ever change that.

That is what separates God from humans.

God never gives up on us.

100. Ways

You have had enough of life – taedium vitae, right?
No. Every moment has a thousand faces to see.
You can explore every moment in thousand ways and it depends on you to choose your ways.
The only thing you need is the will to live life with vigor.

101. Rain

at around 12 o'clock, it started raining
and I prayed to be like that rain
soothing and pleasing to some overthinker.

102. Belief

Don't abandon yourself above all. Do not ever abandon or give up on yourself.

You may fail or feel self-hatred but I promise if you keep believing in yourself there will come a day when you feel peace prevailing inside you; when you will have the ability to move in every storm with a smile and beautiful patience.

It is a sin to give up on yourself and to be hard on yourself. You may be floundering but you are not lost. You will find yourself again all you have to do is keep going with the light God has put inside you.

103. Pain

1.

Don't let pain control you.
Be with pain but don't let pain be with you.
At certain point, let it go.

2.

You will always have to find something higher than the pain you are feeling.
Something like pain that is more painful than your pain.

104. Women of house

a house without woman
silence of such place
a house with women for ages
and a sudden jolt of time
now a house without woman
after ages of harbouring love of
a mother, a sister, a daughter, a wife
now suddenly a house without woman
silence of such house
pours in the hopelessness of an uncared home.
a house full of men
with egos and broken selves
a house of such men
bring hopeless sigh.
a house must go on with broken men -
the new man of post-modern world.
the show must go on with or without woman…
broken could be repaired
home could be rebuild with men
but a child,
still asks for a home with a woman.

105. Loneliness

A level
where you don't scare off a bug in your room and instead start talking to it about things.
Like right now there is a moth right in front of my desk and I am here watching it with so much love.
This dude is all I have got right now.

106. Road

you take a road,
select a destination and try to make the journey memorable,
along the road you make memories
some good and a few bad
you keep imagining the pleasure of reaching your destination
not knowing how things could be during the journey. then
out of nowhere, the road starts playing its tricks. somewhere
it has got a blind curve
one which takes the life out of your lungs
then a bad road follows and almost drives you downhill.
but you go on with the hope of witnessing something
beautiful in the end.
some moments you almost desire and even pray to give up,
to turn around and never look back but something pulls you,
motivates your spirits to soar,
to think about the landscape waiting at the top.
so you carry on, dejected but hopeful,
tired but enthusiastic,
hungry but full of pain to conquer something unattainable to
weak.
you let things work
you let the road take you to a new world of thoughts and
contemplation

you let the peace be your destination and you realize that all the fatigue is worth it, all the worldly suffering is worth that peace.

107. Lost

Many things matter when it comes to finding yourself. The daily brush with complexities of life takes away the ability to feel. I have lately found myself reacting indifferently to situations I come across. Somehow, I have moulded myself into a callous person. I feel everything moving around like wind going around a stone. Suddenly, Earth is immaterial to me. Everybody I love is just a bunch of people to me. I am scared of this thought. I feel suffocation. What if life kills me before I could find some meaning or purpose to live for? This haunts me.

108. Oblivious

You wake up with feelings as you slept with
the same irregularities surrounding you
there ain't any perfection in any moment
there ain't any dream
you develop a habit of not despairing.
you tend to believe in order even when chaos surrounds you.

109. A person

a person who always wants to have dominance and control. one needs to be free like clouds. roam around places and find a land worth raining over.

110. Words

1.

when you love,
do not let joy be yours only,
keep people in your love.
love universal.
love with devotion.
love with selflessness.
look for new ways to love.

2.

love your children
but let them be free
to let them figure out their ways
and never obsess after their affairs.

3.

give whatever you possess
never hoard things
be minimalistic
make use of every small thing you have
never let greed ruin your deed.

4.

respect bread
be humble while eating

keep extra chairs.

5.

work passionately
work gives life meaning
work together.

6.

house built takes time to become home
before you start building a house
be mindful of the coming home.

7.

be free.
cause freedom.

111. Love

I believe you are here very near to me.
All I have to do is reach you and stretch my hand.
I know you will appear and hold it.

9 798889 865261

Printed by Libri Plureos GmbH in Hamburg, Germany